WORKING IN
FASHION

by Mirella S. Miller

12 STORY LIBRARY

www.12StoryLibrary.com

12-Story Library is an imprint of Bookstaves and Press Room Editions

Produced for 12-Story Library by Red Line Editorial

Photographs ©: India Picture/Shutterstock Images, cover, 1; Huang Zheng/Shutterstock Images, 4; TK Kurikawa/Shutterstock Images, 5; Andrea Raffin/Shutterstock Images, 6; Ovidiu Hrubaru/Shutterstock Images, 7, 21; Garry Knight CC2.0, 8; bikeriderlondon/Shutterstock Images, 9; trinetuzun/iStockphoto, 10; Aveda Corporation CC2.0, 11; monkeybusinessimages/iStockphoto, 12; Ted Simpson CC 2.0, 13; Featureflash Photo Agency/Shutterstock Images, 14; Paolo Bona/Shutterstock Images, 15, 29; yuka/ Shutterstock Images, 16; lev radin/Shutterstock Images, 17; Sensay/Shutterstock Images, 18; Monkey Business Images/Shutterstock Images, 19; _jure/iStockphoto, 20, 28; Dragon Images/Shutterstock Images, 22; K2 images/Shutterstock Images, 23; FashionStock.com/Shutterstock Images, 24, 25, 26; Grigory Galantnyy/Shutterstock Images, 27

Library of Congress Cataloging-in-Publication Data
Names: Miller, Mirella S., author.
Title: Working in fashion / by Mirella S. Miller.
Description: Mankato, MN : 12 Story Library, 2017. | Series: Career files | Includes bibliographical references and index. | Audience: Grades 4 to 6.
Identifiers: LCCN 2016047459 (print) | LCCN 2016049714 (ebook) | ISBN 9781632354457 (hardcover : alk. paper) | ISBN 9781632355126 (pbk. : alk. paper) | ISBN 9781621435648 (hosted e-book)
Subjects: LCSH: Fashion--Vocational guidance--Juvenile literature. | Clothing trade--Vocational guidance--Juvenile literature.
Classification: LCC TT507 .M535 2017 (print) | LCC TT507 (ebook) | DDC 746.9/2023--dc23
LC record available at https://lccn.loc.gov/2016047459

Printed in the United States of America
022017

Access free, up-to-date content on this topic plus a full digital version of this book. Scan the QR code on page 31 or use your school's login at 12StoryLibrary.com.

Table of Contents

Fashion Is a Global Industry

Clothes are a part of everyone's daily life. Some clothing protects people. Other clothing serves as a uniform. For most people, clothing is a way to display their personal style. Pieces of clothing can become part of a person's identity.

Fashion is a global market with millions of workers. This huge industry has a variety of jobs to consider. Communication, design, production, and retail are only a few of the broad areas within fashion. It helps to start thinking of a career path within the industry early on. For those going to college, picking a major can determine

Hats are just one accessory people use to express who they are.

future fashion jobs. Some choose to attend colleges that focus on fashion only. Learning more about the industry helps make these decisions.

Some cities around the world are famous for fashion. These fashion capitals include Paris, France; Milan, Italy; London, England; and Tokyo, Japan. In the United States,

Takeshita Street in Harajuku, Tokyo, is famous for Japanese fashion.

New York is the biggest fashion capital. A fashion capital influences fashion trends. Large retail brands, as well as high-end designers, set up shop in these popular cities. This makes a wide variety of clothing available for anyone living in or around these cities.

60 million

Number of people employed by the fashion industry worldwide.

- Clothes can be a part of a person's identity.
- Fashion is a global market with millions of workers.
- New York is the biggest fashion capital in the United States.

Confidence Is the Best Accessory

Every industry and job has traits that are best suited for it. Fashion is no different. Confidence is one of the most important traits a person can have when working in this industry.

The fashion industry can be hard to break into. It is important to be ready for the challenge of finding a good fit. It is common to be rejected many times. But if fashion is a passion, it is important to be persistent. Having confidence in your abilities can help when dealing with rejection.

Being confident can also help in other ways. The fashion industry is focused on body image. Most models are very thin or fit. And photographers, stylists, makeup artists, and designers are constantly surrounded by images of models. The strict standard for models' bodies does not reflect the way the majority of people look. It is common to hear comments about beauty and body shape nonstop. It is

Tom Ford called designer Cathy Hardwick every day for a month, begging for an interview.

68

Percent of the fashion workforce who are women.

- Confidence is one of the most important traits to have when entering the fashion industry.
- Many people are told no before finding a job.
- The fashion industry is very focused on body image.
- Being outgoing and having an open mind will help in this creative field.

important to learn not to take these comments to heart. Everyone's body is different.

Even supermodel Liu Wen was pressured to have plastic surgery on her eyes.

Another trait that will help when trying to break into fashion is being outgoing. In an industry where it's necessary to stand out, it helps to be charismatic. The fashion world is made up of many creative people. It's necessary to have an open mind and be open to new experiences. When looking for leaders, many companies will seek an outgoing person.

THINK ABOUT IT

Imagine you have an interview with a fashion company. Create a list of questions for your interview. How would you show that you are a confident person?

Interns Need to Do Hard Work

There are many jobs to choose from within the fashion industry. But they all call for hard work. Internships in fashion are generally unpaid. The experience interns gain is the most important thing. Fashion companies look for experience when hiring full-time employees.

Interns may want to think twice before wearing uncomfortable shoes. Typical duties include running errands, making deliveries, and hauling gowns and garment bags around. Lifting heavy boxes of clothing isn't unusual. Some interns spend much of their time running to events. They may bounce from event

Interns outside London Fashion Week

17

Hours per day an intern often works during New York Fashion Week.

- All jobs within the fashion world require hard work.
- Most fashion internships are unpaid.
- Running errands is a big part of internships.
- Being willing to work long hours and work with a team are important qualities.

to event during the day.

Interns need to be willing to work long hours. Sometimes this means working more than five days a week, too. An internship with a designer can be especially busy leading up to New York Fashion Week.

Some interns measure fabric for fashion designers.

Some work in the fashion world is done alone. But much of it is done together as a team. Public relations firms often help run fashion events and shows. It takes a large group of people to get this done. Being friendly and willing to take on any task will help an intern make a good impression.

Creativity Is Key

4

Most people who work in fashion are creative. Creativity can mean different things. It may mean being good at drawing or matching colors and patterns. Creativity can also be having good problem-solving skills. It means coming up with new ideas and methods.

Fashion designers work with many fabrics, shapes, colors, and patterns. They must make all of these things work together. Creating new and distinct pieces of clothing is a big part

Designers sometimes use a mood board to start the creative process.

of their job. And without their creativity, there would be no clothing.

Stylists have to figure out how to put it all together. They think about what accessories look best with certain outfits. Some trends aren't about new clothes but rather new ways to wear them. Stylists put together many different looks to see what works.

Photographers take pictures that make people want to buy products. To do this, they use tools such as lighting and props to create a mood. They arrange objects to make people feel certain emotions. Photographers tell stories with their pictures.

Makeup artists use eyeshadow, mascara, lipstick, and other tools to change the way models look.

STEVEN ALAN S/S 2014

BRUSH THRU W/CACAO

LIGHT MOSSCARA

CENTER OF LID DAB PEONY BLUSH

PRESS IN W/ FINGER TIPS BURNISHED BRONZE

LIGHTLY CONTOURED CHEEKS

SHEER MUSCADINE AS A STAIN PRESSED IN

SKIN: FRESH, HEALTHY, LUMINOUS

20
Number of photos fashion photographers should have in their portfolios.

- The fashion industry is full of creative people.
- Fashion designers work with many fabrics, shapes, colors, and patterns.
- Stylists use accessories to create a complete look.
- Photographers create moods and emotions in pictures that make people want to buy products.

THINK ABOUT IT

Imagine you have to create a magazine ad for a new pair of shoes. What tools would you use to make people want to buy them? What moods or emotions should your picture create?

11

Getting Schooled in Fashion

A college degree isn't a requirement to enter the fashion industry. But having one can mean more available job opportunities. Taking special courses can help students make connections with important people in the industry. This can lead to internships or jobs.

Many professors have worked in the fashion industry.

There are hundreds of different options to choose from when getting a degree. Fashion schools are located around the world. Students must pick a college that feels like the best fit for them. Some students may be more design

Many fashion schools offer classes on garment construction.

6

Percentage of applicants who are accepted to Central Saint Martins fashion school in London, England.

- Having a college degree is not required but can be helpful.
- There are hundreds of different courses to take within a fashion degree.
- Degrees vary from design to marketing.
- There are top fashion schools around the world.

Parsons was founded in 1896.

PARSONS THE NEW SCHOOL FOR DESIGN

Parsons The New School for Design is located in New York City. Many people recognize it from the TV show *Project Runway*. It is near hundreds of fashion internships. Many famous designers graduated from Parsons, including Donna Karan, Marc Jacobs, and Tom Ford.

focused, studying fashion design or costume design. Or they may have a broader focus on the industry. Other students choose to focus on merchandising, marketing, and social media.

Some people want to learn more about the industry before choosing a job. Attending a school like the Fashion Institute of Technology (FIT) might be a good option. It offers a mix of degrees that take between two to four years to earn. Some famous people who have attended the school include designer Michael Kors and journalist Nina Garcia.

Those looking to become fashion writers and editors should

think about earning a degree in journalism. Some choices include Syracuse University and the Columbia Graduate School of Journalism. Many people who work in public relations first earn degrees in journalism.

13

Stylists Create a Head-to-Toe Look

Many celebrities are photographed every day. Their entire appearance is examined. People look at celebrities' clothes, shoes, accessories, hair, and makeup. To keep it all together, most celebrities hire a stylist.

Stylists work with different people in the fashion industry to create a look for their clients. Most celebrities want to project a certain image. Stylists have to figure out how to use certain clothes, shoes, and makeup to create that image. Designers often send clothes to stylists, hoping they'll use them to dress celebrities.

One of the most well-known stylists is Rachel Zoe. She has styled Miley Cyrus and Jennifer Lawrence. Zoe has no formal training in styling but is very passionate about it. This has led to a successful career.

Kate Young is another top stylist. She once worked at *Vogue* and has styled Natalie Portman and

Rachel Zoe

Stylists help the makeup and hair stylists get the right look for a runway show.

Selena Gomez. Young is known for making her clients feel fashionable and comfortable.

Stylists frequently work with designers and public relations companies. At fashion shows, they help create a unified look with all the clothes and models. During photo shoots, they work with hair and makeup professionals. Stylists make sure a model's shoes, hair, and makeup complement the designer's clothes.

$50,346
Average salary for a fashion stylist.

- Celebrities want a signature look and hire stylists to create it.
- Stylists work with designers to pick out clothes, shoes, and other accessories for their clients.
- Stylists work at fashion shows and photo shoots to create a complete look.

Fashion Is More Than Images

Communication is a big part of the larger fashion industry. Writers tell stories. That's how people outside the fashion world find out about designers, photographers, and models. Many trends are formed and spread because of articles or blog posts. Designers and retailers must work with writers to have their stories told.

Fashion journalists write articles on events, people, and clothing. They may write for a newspaper or a magazine, such as *Elle* or *Vogue*. Fashion blogs are popular, and anyone can start one. Journalists cover everything from New York

Journalists have to take notes during fashion shows.

18.5 million
Number of people who read *Vogue*.

- Communication is a big part of the fashion industry.
- Designers and retailers must work with writers.
- Fashion journalists write about events, people, and news.
- Editors are in control of a publication.

Anna Wintour (center) is one of the most famous artistic directors in fashion.

Fashion Week to celebrity style to news about retail companies. Some articles can be about something as big as a designer's fall collection. Other articles can be about a single item, such as mascara or boots. It is a writer's job to provide the text for a story. This means doing research and interviews.

Editors pick and choose the stories that will be covered in a publication. They are in control and often select an overall theme.

ART AND CREATIVE DIRECTORS

There are other jobs in journalism where words aren't as important. Art and creative directors help tell stories through images. They may help with an advertising campaign or set up a photo shoot for a story. Art directors work with many different people. They have to be good at translating ideas into pictures.

They also choose the best images to run with the text. Editors make sure stories are perfect before publishing them.

17

Retail Sells the Goods

Retail is a big business that is always changing. Fashion retail includes many types of stores and jobs. Department stores, chain stores, boutiques, thrift stores, outlets, catalogs, and Internet stores all sell fashion. And all of these stores must keep up with trends to meet their customers' needs.

Most jobs in retail are in sales and customer service. Sales assistants make sure the store floor is clean and presentable. They check stock on items and refill missing sizes. They also spend time working at the cash register. A big part of the job is making customers happy. Store managers are in charge of all sales people. Owners of small stores or boutiques may do all these jobs.

Fashion buyers work for retailers and work with designers. Usually their job is to buy large quantities

Sales assistants return clothes left in dressing rooms to make sure stores look clean and neat.

Buyers meet with fashion designers.

of a specific item of clothing, such as denim. Buyers help designers get their creations into stores. And buyers make sure stores have the right amount of clothing at the right prices.

Merchandisers work in stores. They try to understand what customers will purchase during each season. They tell buyers what to look for. They try not to have leftover clothing at the end of a season.

$250 billion

Amount of money spent on fashion in the United States every year.

- Fashion retail includes many types of stores and jobs.
- Most jobs are in sales and customer service positions.
- Sales assistants work to make customers happy.
- Fashion buyers work with designers and retailers.

The Business of Spotting and Creating Trends

Much of the fashion world is focused on design, but the industry also has a business side. Forecasters play an important part. They track trends and try to guess what will be popular in upcoming seasons. They give this information to designers. Thinking about what people will want helps designers when making their creations. Forecasters watch celebrities, art, music, movies, and other things to make their decisions.

People in public relations help companies build awareness around their brands. They might send clothing or accessories to celebrities or stylists. When a celebrity wears the item, it is free advertising. Public relations people also make sure publications have positive stories

Forecasters try to figure out which colors and fabrics will be popular next season.

75,000

Number of customers who pay the World's Global Style Network to forecast fashion trends.

- Forecasters guess what trends will be popular in upcoming seasons.
- Public relations people help companies build awareness.
- Public relations is a stressful and busy job.
- It helps to be organized and good at solving problems.

SOCIAL MEDIA

Those looking to start a career in public relations should first look at their own social media profiles. Developing a polished personal brand shows many of the same skills needed to create a company's brand. Follow key fashion companies and their competitors on social media. Connections made online can lead to job offers.

on the brands. They have to build relationships with fashion editors.

Public relations can be stressful. It is a busy schedule. People in public relations help put on parties, events, and runway shows. It is their job to make sure everyone else is having fun. They have to be creative and quickly solve problems that pop up during events. It is helpful for someone working in public relations to be very organized.

A public relations team sent Zoe Saldana this Dolce & Gabbana gown to wear to the Met Gala in 2016.

Designers Are the Heart of Fashion

Fashion designer is the most well-known job in the fashion industry. But there are many types of designers. It helps to have an idea of what path to take. There are three broad areas: haute couture, ready-to-wear, and mass market. Haute couture is very expensive and made by hand. Ready-to-wear clothing is designed for most runway shows and boutiques. Mass market clothing is sold at shopping mall stores.

Designers may also choose to specialize in women's, men's, or children's clothing. Undergarments and activewear are other areas.

Designers sometimes try to match colors exactly.

Some designers work on wedding dresses. There are designers who create only accessories. They design jewelry, shoes, or purses.

Designers are creative people. They spend between 6 weeks to 18 months on their work. Designers have to be good at visual translation. They have to figure out how to include their inspirations without copying anyone else's work. They may create their designs alone or with a team.

Finalists on *Project Runway* present their collections at New York Fashion Week.

6,000
Number of hours it took to hand sew an Elie Saab wedding dress.

- Fashion designer is the most well-known job in the industry.
- Broad areas include haute couture, ready-to-wear, and mass market.
- Women's, men's, and children's are just some of the areas to choose from.
- Some designers work on accessories.

PROJECT RUNWAY

For more than 10 years, people have watched *Project Runway*. The reality show features amateur fashion designers who compete for a prize of $100,000. The show highlights some important fashion places in New York, such as Mood Fabrics. For viewers, *Project Runway* offers a behind-the-scenes look at the long hours designers must work to create their clothing.

Fashion Week Takes Place around the World

New York is one of the biggest fashion capitals in the United States. Twice a year, people involved in the industry gather for Fashion Week. The most popular designers host runway shows to present their newest collections. The runway shows debut the upcoming trends for the year. Fashion Week in February features clothes for the fall and winter. Fashion Week in September shows off collections for next year's spring and summer. Editors get ideas to feature on their blogs or in their magazines.

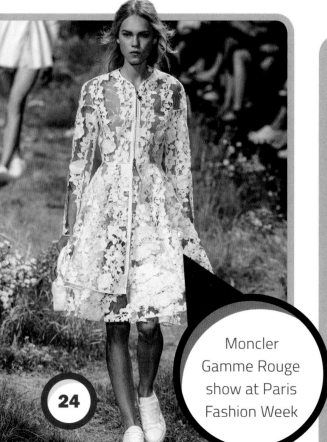

Moncler Gamme Rouge show at Paris Fashion Week

40

Average number of outfits shown during a runway show.

- Fashion Week happens every February and September.
- The most popular designers present their collections for the upcoming season.
- Fashion Week takes place in New York, London, Milan, and Paris.
- It is an important week for everyone in the industry.

Backstage at New York Fashion Week

Buyers can decide what to buy for their stores.

But Fashion Week doesn't end once the New York shows are over. Fashion Week moves on to London and then Milan. Fashion Week finally ends with shows in Paris.

Fashion Week isn't just for the designers. It is also important for models and hair and makeup professionals. Some runway shows use famous models. Others use models who are just starting their careers. Hundreds of models walk the runways during the week. For some models, walking in a high-profile runway show leads to more work.

HISTORY OF FASHION WEEK

Fashion shows have their roots in France. But the first Fashion Week took place in New York in 1943 during World War II. It was called Press Week. The American fashion media could not travel to Paris because of the war. So the US designers wanted to show the world what they could do. Press Week was the first time several runway shows were grouped together during a particular time. But it wasn't until the 1990s that the shows were all held mostly under one roof.

Fashion Going Forward

Fashion is an always-changing industry. Trends come and go. Social media has transformed the industry.

Social media applications allow the fashion industry to spot which trends are popular with followers on the site. Designers use social media to debut outfit ideas and new collections. Celebrities use social media to tease what they will be wearing to awards shows. Some followers of these accounts want to match the trends they see. Designer Mary Katrantzou once posted a photo of a minidress that

Designer Roberto Cavalli likes to use social media to give a sneak peak of what he'll be sending down the runway.

THINK ABOUT IT

Brainstorm different ways fashion could be more ethical. Pick one idea and then write a letter to a fashion designer explaining your ideas.

1,083

Number of gallons (5,000 L) of water needed to create one T-shirt.

- Social media has changed the fashion industry.
- Followers want to match trends they see online.
- Retail companies and designers are working to make fashion more environmentally friendly.

Stella McCartney

cost $8,680. She quickly sold three that same day.

But the fashion industry, unfortunately, is often a source of pollution. It uses many natural resources. Animal products, water, dyes, and chemicals are all used to create clothing. People in the United States throw away 13 million tons (12 million metric t) of clothes every year. Designers and companies are starting to pay more attention to these ethical problems. Levi's is working to make their denim production more water-efficient. Retail giant H&M has promised to use only recycled or organic cotton in

their clothing by 2020. And designer Stella McCartney uses no animal products, instead finding alternate materials for leather.

Other Jobs to Consider

Jewelry Designer

Description: Create, manufacture, and sell jewelry pieces
Training/Education: High school diploma
Outlook: In decline
Average salary: $37,060

Graphic Designer

Description: Use computer programs to create advertisements, brochures, magazines, and other communication pieces
Training/Education: Bachelor's degree
Outlook: Steady
Average salary: $46,900

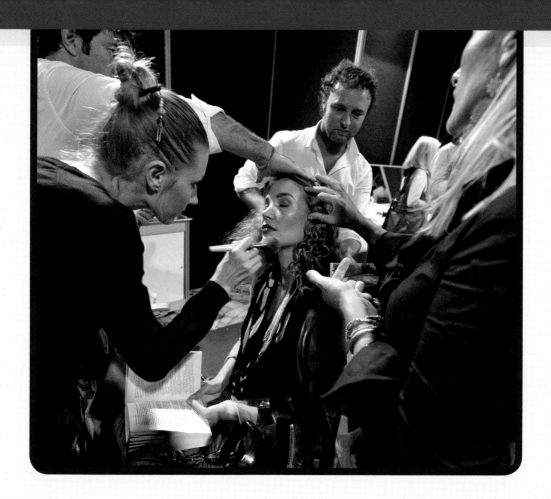

Model

Description: Pose for photographs to help advertise products and walk in runway shows

Training/Education: No formal education needed

Outlook: Steady

Average salary: $27,530

Photographer

Description: Take photographs and tell stories through images

Training/Education: High school diploma

Outlook: Steady

Average salary: $31,710

Glossary

amateur
Someone who isn't a professional.

boutique
A small store that sells expensive clothing and other goods.

collection
A group of outfits or objects created by a designer during a season.

ethical
Morally right and good.

industry
A group of businesses that provides a particular service or product.

intern
A student or recent graduate who works for a certain time to gain experience.

merchandising
The activity of trying to sell goods by advertising them.

portfolio
A selection of photographs collected in a folder.

production
The process of making something for sale.

public relations
The relationship between a company and the public.

rejection
The action of refusing someone acceptance, a job, or a position.

For More Information

Books

Joicey, Celia, and Dennis Nothdruft. *How to Draw like a Fashion Designer*. New York: Thames & Hudson, 2013.

Kallen, Stuart. *Careers If You Like the Arts*. San Diego, CA: ReferencePoint, 2017.

Kelley, K. C., and John Willis. *Fashion Design Secrets*. New York: AV2, 2017.

Visit 12StoryLibrary.com

Scan the code or use your school's login at **12StoryLibrary.com** for recent updates about this topic and a full digital version of this book. Enjoy free access to:

- Digital ebook
- Breaking news updates
- Live content feeds
- Videos, interactive maps, and graphics
- Additional web resources

Note to educators: Visit 12StoryLibrary.com/register to sign up for free premium website access. Enjoy live content plus a full digital version of every 12-Story Library book you own for every student at your school.

Index

About the Author

Mirella S. Miller is an author and editor of several children's books. She lives in Minnesota with her husband and their dog.